THE
TRUTH
IS
WE
ARE
PERFECT

THE
TRUTH
IS
WE
ARE
PERFECT

JANAKA STUCKY

THIRD MAN BOOKS
NASHVILLE, TENNESSEE

TO ACCESS JANAKA STUCKY RECORDED LIVE AT TMR:

http://www.thirdmanbooks.com/janakatruth
password: WeAreAllPerfect_2015

Printed in Nashville, Tennessee

Library of Congress Control Number: 2015931193

FIRST EDITION
Design by Nathanio Strimpopulos
Cover illustration by Josh Wallis

ISBN   978-0-9913361-1-1

TABLE OF CONTENTS

THE WORLD WILL DENY IT FOR YOU

YOUR NAME IS THE ONLY FREEDOM

RECREATING A MIRACULOUS OBJECT

The renunciation of desire is the renunciation of the world.
Now you may live anywhere.

—The Ashtavakra Gita

RECREATING A MIRACULOUS OBJECT

Belonging not to winter but to another
I face the face that made me

And lie all my hours
Upon your reckless hands

Make myself a prisoner
Of the sky

The sweet vermouth
Of your teeth

Shaping me
Like a spectre

In the attic of my flowering heart

I hear the parade of mouths
Beating upon my sleeping head

I hear the thieves rising
With their fingers full of moon

I hear the ocean I gave you
Waving back against the black

Uniform of the earth
And the saint children marching

Like blood

I hear your memories of me waken
And glisten

And rise in the hollow
Of my muscled dread

Treading through the unlatched snow
Here they come

Here they come
Here come my betrayers

THE
WORLD
WILL
DENY
IT
FOR
YOU

EVERYONE THINKS I'M ANCIENT
BUT I'M ONLY SEVEN

In the hundred years it takes to cross the ocean between us, I read every book in my body. I said goodbye tonight, to Antarctica, as the lightning picked up. All my maps are useless and invisible. Every now and then a tentacle reaches up from the darkness and points to the places you are not. In my dreams I remember everything about you, but when I wake there is only your hair in my fists and the journey ahead. I imagine when my small boat finally arrives, the angel in your place will say that I am too late—you are long gone. And when I tell him it's been a hundred years he will laugh and say it's only been seven days and his mouth will grow wide and he will swallow me whole.

THE ART OF LOSS IS A LOST ART

Because I love a burning thing
I made my heart a field of fire

In this way I own nothing
Can lose nothing

The moon cake you fed me remains
A ghost upon my tongue

Immortal wasp
Tiny white flame I have never touched

The truth is
We are perfect

Hours unspent like diamonds
In the invisible now

Without each other
Still we are perfect

I make with my mouth
The hour of your arrival

Again and again
In my indefinite sleep

THE WORLD WILL BE DESOLATE
BUT ADAM OF LIGHT WILL SHINE FORTH

Resolve to live in a state of desire

Touch everyone you encounter and know
You touch nothing

                Become androgynous
Extract your rib and fuck yourself with it and beget
Seven androgynous children who will sleep with themselves and
Beget seven more

                      Hide in the woods
                      Turn into the trees
                      The trees will die

           Eventually you will live in the desert

Your forty-nine children will become the forty-nine winds
Your rib will be consumed by a vulture
And you will walk fiercely unto the sun until the sun itself turns away

You will tremble

Everything will shake

And you will tremble

YOU ARE INVISIBLE. GO VISIBLE.

Inside the mouth of the flower remains
The second eyelid
      True darkness

Alien light

Resurrecting us
Slender and thickskinned

From the pool of milk we drown in each morning
From the river of moth dust we float on at night

Hand in invisible hand saying
Go and be

Build your impossible fort full of secret magics
Designed to let others in

THE HEART WILL BE DESTROYED TO GIVE PLACE TO THE LIGHT WHICH IT MIGHT HAVE CONTAINED

Nothing cannot pass
Through me the mask
I wear is a pyramid of fire

Fierce geometry of light

A cloud and its shadow
The hesitation of a lightning bolt

Watch my face ignite
With every no

Watch me become
Invisible as I guard the yes
You left behind

     Watch me poltergeist as I
     Chrysalis your life
          In my long hollow *boOOoOoo*

Think of my white hands
Haunting any house you build

And my broad pale chest
Loving you   with my ghost heart
Until I am no longer dead

THE CONCEPT OF OUR GREAT POWER

Under a white sky we stand
In a vast pasture of black tentacles

Enduring the aeon
Of invisible age

Kindless wonder we keep
Tucked blindly under a belt of knives

But now is here
This massacre of breath

Erupting from our hands'
Collision the moment we see

Instead of the sun
Up from the world's edge

An exaltation of tongues
Crack the firmament

While the creatured earth hums
Us two too

Mute as shellfish
Falling backward in

To our bodies fractured
With love we sing

All flesh is flesh
A quivering of fins

SANSKRIT

In the forest
Your arms around my neck
Toe gripping dust

Even now years later when the deer remember it
Leaves drop from their mouths

I HOPE TO COME TO YOU WITH NOTHING BUT LIGHT

If I had a finger for every time I breathed
I'd be a planet of angels

Mild suffering
Secret invisible wonder

I exhale my doubt and wait

In the shadow of hope against hope I speak
To every bodypart that rebels to be with me

Dear your hands
Which I have never held
Sieve the light from my approach

Dear white thigh
Growing whiter in my absence
Night sky shudder against my cheek

Dear soft sigh
The mystery I guess
As though there might contain my own heart

Dear your tongue
Let me see you for

The days grow short now
The jellyfish bloom and

We never don't know anything
About someone

HELL MUST EXIST A GREAT PRIEST SAID SO

The terrible mountain of needles
A lake of blood souls with human faces
Grow four legs and fall into

All the things we've ever done

Have brought us to this very point

It could have been different   but not really

And besides

It isn't

How does it feel to think about anything at all?

The hour you lost your virginity

Every blink of your eyes

The quiet heaving that is living moment to moment
And every moment leading to this

Wherever you are

When I have a memory
I see my destroyer

Love at third sight
The world is drowning

The world has drowned
We are drowning

We are drowned
We are drowned

THE GRENADE, A BIRD

And your vagina next to me sleeping

        Cicadas sing their mating calls and the Cicada Killer comes

Bacon with our eggs   Honey
In the tea   You
Fuck me dead   A day later

The ground is full of penis

The children will raise their palms to your mouth. The children will feed you rare bananas with black meat. Bananas they stole from the garden of the old Child Eater, braving his wild hair and wicked claws. Braving the screams of the Child Eater as they ran, clutching sweet impossibly black fruit, with tears streaming. Brave little children, wicked things, who only want magic in their own sticky hands. Who believe in you until there's nothing left, called home to dinner. You're just a horn in the gutter. No princess to save you, no spells. Your remaining days turn out to be many many years.

WE ARE NOT EMPTY WE CAST SPELLS

I make with my open palms
The ghost of an iron book

The better to fold your atoms with

I hold it up

To the light that is not there

And wait like this forever

ELEGY

My musclememory of her
Open palm is to close
My eyes   Breathe rapidly

The Leopard People of Sierra Leone carry their dead in a bag
Whenever they feel sorrow they cut off a piece and eat it

EACH A THREADLESS DISTANCE
FROM CROW AND LINEAMENT

And all the phone lines down
The snow is up to our knees again
So we stay in our separate rooms
Read the twitches in our fibers
The truly great books

Every person is afraid
Of every person

Watching the sky for something
We are not capable of

We call each snowflake
Epic   like heroin
And our addiction buries us

A few seconds of silents

What is the winter for
Why does it bury the tracks
        When there is nothing on the other side of the tracks

Why you won't speak to me
When all we are
Are tongues

YOU FIND BEAUTY IN ORDINARY THINGS
DO NOT LOSE THIS ABILITY

Document the moment my thumb and index
Finger first cradled your jaw

I eat cold eel
Think distant thoughts

I create the oracle

When the oracle says you
I punch the sun   my fists impervious
To flame on account
Of all the love I keep stuffed in their knuckles

When you are away
You are not away

When your body does not contain me
Your distance contains no absence

There is nothing wrong with being alive

Ascend to the mountain top and hover

While eagles and angels copulate
In the air around
Our snow-laden bodies of light

I feel like I was always meant to be

You find beauty in ordinary things

Do not lose me
Do not lose me

THERE WAS A MONSTER BUT I NEVER SAW HIM

My bruised body
Saw you off
In to nothing

The moment you arrived you were
Already leaving   After you left

I found an angel's canine
The size of a man beneath my bed

JENNIFER. BLOOD.

Beneath the olive tree
Your tongue   interrogating blade
Slips across my skin

In the grass

My hieroglyphic fucking
When I forget how to say I love you

The crop of stones beside us moves closer
Down

The only word left is your name
Your name
An ocean of black magic between us

We spend the night with your finger in my mouth
        My favorite pen in your ribs

At dawn
You quiver above me   fall
Rise up burning

YOU WILL KNOW HER DISAPPEARANCE

You will know her disappearance
By the knife left upon your pillow's case

A corpse with its hand
Stuck in a beehive

Glacier of blood

You will count the nights apart
On your remaining fingers

In the wet cave of your loneliness
You will spoon the knife against your naked frame

You will dream of the knife standing
At the window like she used to

And the knife will become her in a phosphorescent dress
And she will become the moon in the black sky
And the moon will leave you

YOU MUST GO BY THE WAY OF DISPOSSESSION

On your way out hand me your skin
It has my fingerprints all over it

While you're at it leave your hair
Your hair   your hair
Breasts O my heart

      Then place in me the object of your disgrace

         Fall into another

Hold him between your thighs until you cough bulimic Iloveyous

Deny yourself nothing
The world will deny it for you

Come knowing my memory of happiness
Is not you

Or what we had

But that afternoon on the hill

The dry leaves and your teeth

THE OPPOSITE OF DREAMS

Every lover is a home and what is architecture
A place which is nothing and indistinguishable
From all the other nothing until we place it
By placing something in it   and thus experience time

The architecture of my past is slipping away
I walk from room to empty room and fill each
One with miscellany   nights and teardrops
Piling in the corners of every mouth I've kissed

Memories are the opposite
Of dreams   which are placeless

Your hands are a bungalow by the lake
Our child is a vulture   a black speck in the white sky

All these things we don't have circle our house at night

My nightmares of our burning bedroom   The things I would save

THIS IS THE HOUR WHEN YOU LEARN TO LOVE WITHOUT

No this is

No this is

No this is no this is

MOVE THE BACK OF YOUR HEART
TOWARDS THE FRONT OF YOUR HEART

We have become
White-blooded people of the future

Let me show you pictures of the man
I was when I was

Other than the man
I am right now

I have always wanted to be looked at
The way you look at me when I move

The back of my heart toward
The front of my heart

      The parenthesis of light
      Along your eye's rim

Unbuttons me to the crescent shore of now
I break upon each time I land

At last

The solace of the world's worst thing

YOUR
NAME
IS
THE
ONLY
FREEDOM

BASK IN THE ETERNAL FLAME
OF THE EYE OF THE IMMORTAL

Make nothing your own which comes
From another

When a tree grows in your yard you must
Eventually decide whether to chop it or move

These are your only options

If you chop the tree down
Burn it to stay warm

If you move then burn it while standing   Bask
In the eternal flame of the eye of the immortal

Let your empty hands remain empty

Let your footsteps begin with ash

Lay your future head upon the pillow I wove you
Of all the matter we stripped from light

I WAS A TEENAGE SYMPHONY TO GOD

I was

A choir of burning stars
Two hundred volcanoes erupting human blood

I was one thousand
Tortoises dryly writhing
In a field of my mother's dark hair

I was the body of a man with the head of an ox
I was the white path between water and fire

I was covered in honey
I was the fly

I was the tornado from a butterfly's wing
Halfway across the world
I was the world

I was the ocean
The jellyfish
The pine tree
The needles
The fly

(I was covered in honey)

That bit you
Holding you in its belly

I was holding you in its belly
I was you as you became the plague
I was the plague
I was the spider
That swallowed the fly

Perhaps I'll die

DESTROY SONG

I am dead
My body is still dying

I am dead but
My body is still dying

I am
Dead my body is still dying

I am dead but my body is
Still dying

I am dead my body is still
Dying

DEATH DOES NOT DIMINISH ME

My broken neck singing

A holocaust of seahorses

Every bone become an island
Every mouth become a sea

A piece of a piece of nothing
What kills me only makes me

WE ARE PURIFIED AS APOCALYPTIC SIGNS
APPEAR

The night you wake up sobbing
Throw yourself upon my chest
For wickedness has become stronger than you
Helpless and alone are the nights

The stars will expand and the moon will stop shining

Next are darkness
Wind and a moment
Long as the closing of an eye

I ask you if there is an other
You meet me with silence

Fold your fingers into mine
Wash my body with your hair

Every breath has been a footstep into death
Each footstep brought us closer into this immeasurable light

WHERE INSECT SHADOWS WAR

Without apology vibrate
Awake the sleeping heat

In the dark there is only darkness and
The darker things dark clings to

Your naked body
Arched and
Full of wounds

The black sky
With veins
Of blacker trees running through it

Scissors flocked and cooing
Along the bark

Everywhere we don't look within
This enormous waiting room

      Children play with matches
      Planes about to crash

      My vampire skin is drowning

In the bed of this dumb animal skull
My butcher's eye hums
With the one breath I've left

THE SEVEN HEAVENS OF CHAOS

The eclipse of my hand
On your mouth your moan
A cold halo radiating around the edge

Your hips rising to meet me again
And again like the tide or the pressure of blood

What little light there is
Burning   in your eyes like a witch

We have always been here
      Killing each other

The ones we abandoned growing
Into a forest around us fertilized
With sweat and cum
      You reach for the nearest one

Hang all possibility
By its neck
From a limb

No ascension
No collapse

The world upon us like a plague of insects
We catch

One scaly wing at a time

DESTROY SONG

I want to make a cut
That will sing

How you breathe
Next to me blood

Whistling and turned
To ice by the time it hits

The ground

SUICIDE BALM

Your lipstick strapped tightly to my chest
I run into a crowded restaurant
And plug it in

OPPOSED AND PERSECUTED IN THE WORLD

Your laughter rises from our bed
In the dark and produces wings and flies
From the ceiling to the window and out
Into the street beyond the tree we planted
Up over the roofs of every house without
Lamb's blood upon the door taking

The breath from the firstborns' mouths with it as it grows
Larger than the memory of night the tears in our eyes
Moistening the pillows as we finally have our revenge

I'M A FOOL WHO ARE YOU

All these minutes I thought joy was enough
Now you're a stranger with teeth touching mine

Our honest desire will eventually destroy us

In the meantime let's stand in the shadows
Give each other new names that mean nothing
Let the shroud of ecstatic nonsense cover us

Blindly we map
The latitude   Take notes

      On the proper way to
      Grip a knife

When you begin my world buckles into
Jagged invisibles

Your skin glows like a sidewalk in the dark
Your mouth an alley with my murder inside

DESTROY SONG

You make wishes on my lost hair
When you cry

Hurricane of lashes
I am in the eye

THE FIFTH KINGDOM CREATED A SOUL OF BLOOD

Missionary upon you you
Lay your palms upon
My wings of bone

Unfolding beneath
The entirety against you you
      Sway upwards

        Buck like fuck as I press
           My hand between your breasts

My fingertip assassins
Surround your palace of blood

You come crying
A swarm of insects

      Up from the abyss

The King is dead

Long live the King

HOLY AFFIRMING HOLY DENYING

My body is white with ash
I move slowly

Approaching your black
Body detonating

Indistinguishable against the night

       I reach for your hair but touch the hair of another

My white fingertips growing dark as they run across
The garland of severed heads you wear around your neck

         Still
         Holy
         Holy

Facing me while I close the lid of every eye
You sigh

I AM NOT WORTHY TO PRONOUNCE
THE NAME OF THE ONE WHO HAS SENT YOU

When your breath breaks like a wave
On my skin I become

Naked and imperishable

Reduce me now to ashes   *Amen*
Night like a black sun   *Amen Amen*

DESTROY SONG

I have no face
But I remember that being said

I have no face but I have heard that
Said before

FOR WHOEVER HAS A NAME
HAS BEEN MADE BY ANOTHER

The flag I stake atop
The mountain of her absence bears
A hand forever
Waiving in the high wind

      Call this place desire

For arctic gulls fuck here
Often

      Lay eggs   disappear

Their hollow bones weigh less than snow

To be quiet is to be released
To be named is to be made by another

To be tread upon by your black feet
Is to be a god

Is to be
Is to be

Is to play possum so that I might drown beneath the blood that drips
From your unnamable tongue

THERE IS NO I IN FUNERAL

The coffin a palindrome

Frail tub of water you could reach into
Make a fist and drain
The starlight in my blood

There is no I in funeral
I   solitary glyph
I   a suture stretched across the page
I   the inevitable

Blessing of death   In death
I blossom   Send bouquets

Celebrate death like you would life
Buy yourself new shoes
Go out to dinner take a walk

Everyone has their own ways of keeping company

In the end there is no end just the first day
Of the rest of your life

A flock of waxwings in the rowan tree is
Evidence of a successful crossing

According to tradition it is best to return in the form of a bird

WHAT IS MY DECISION TO DIE

Burn all my books thinking of the magnets in your hands
Across the frozen water I ghost

HOPEFUL IN SPITE OF LEGION

Of beasts of blood
　　　Of devils of horrid hell

Of appetites & passions

Of wickedness of the mighty wickedness
That sleeps in another's hair

Of giving away your heart when it is no longer
Yours alone to give

　　　Of neglect the jabberwocky
　　　Of snicker snack

Of the souring light the preserving night
Of the mushrooms we find there

　　　Of poison

Hopeful in spite of spite

Of wakefulness the reach of my arm
　　　Of the space beside me that no longer grows warm

Of denial of denial of denial

Of the steady hand
That traces the silhouette
Of the moment you left
Not the body
But the place
It inhabits
Still breathing
Every breath
Hope

A MATCHBOX WITH BEETLE WINGS INSIDE

Everyday take something you've found

To be beautiful and send it somewhere else
So that when you're alone in your room

Sitting crosslegged and wondering
Who will feed everyone you love

You can look back at those things those things
You have willingly lost and say

At least I don't have that

WE RECEIVE THE WORD HOLY

Rejoice in the destruction of happiness

Om kring Kali om

Fire surround me forever alone

Om kring Kali om

I love you I love you I love you I love you

Om kring Kali om

Your name is the only freedom

Om kring Kali om

RECREATING
A
MIRACULOUS
OBJECT

RECREATING A MIRACULOUS OBJECT

I have lived through every war in my lifetime
Like everyone I am

A vessel that takes the shape
Of what it contains

If you feed me to fire
I will become fire

Place your teeth upon me and I will be
The sound from your mouth

You see that axe that axe
Is me

Cleaving myself from my self
In your hands which are
Also me

When you arrive
I become you coming

The snow you came in
The next great war

I live through

RECREATING A MIRACULOUS OBJECT

Emerging from the mass of shadows
Which make the spitblack night I wear

The white whale of your possibility
Around my neck

From my bed of phantoms
Yours is the hand that grips me tight

Raises me and casts me
Like a spell into the prenatal dawn

Where I hum and hum and hum
And hum

RECREATING A MIRACULOUS OBJECT

When I was a boy I was made
Entirely of salt

Silent with the silence of adoration
For what had come

Before me

Like a father

In the belly of a great whale
I lived in myself

Waiting to be
Illuminated by your arrival

At night I pray
For glaciers of salt

Now I wait
I have waited
I will wait

I eat your footsteps in my sleep
I wake from my animal dream a legend

RECREATING A MIRACULOUS OBJECT

Mine is the tongue
That formed the words
That make you obey

Yours is the neck
A fountain revealing

The inexplicable tenderness

When the descent becomes
Greater than the ascent you

Say I can have you
But you need me

Not to

      Turn my body into smoke

While I wait   for the blackout   you push
My knuckle deeper towards
The back of your throat

RECREATING A MIRACULOUS OBJECT

I lay the cheeks of all my future lovers

Against yours

And am drowned

RECREATING A MIRACULOUS OBJECT

The world pisses on itself and takes
A million forms

The way winter melts and reminds
Us we're alone

Each drop of water punctuating
Our open mouths

Broken by absence but more
Beautiful for it

I want to be a part of all
Things I am apart of

Weave my nest from the teeth
Of laughter

And place it like a crown
Upon your departure's giant brow

I am less
Than an insect moving

From judgment to awe in all things

I am dust
On a moth

The whole universe
Printed on the wings of a moth

RECREATING A MIRACULOUS OBJECT

Ruthlessly we awaken
To shatter the dark uncoiling

Upon our upturned faces

I love you like there is nothing
Else to love

Your closed fist opens me

Like lightning revealing
From sand the secret of glass

And all my limbs are burning
In the bright shafts of forgetting

This miraculous object flowering
Naked in the terrible

Great storm of light

I am a new prison
Announced by your wandering heart

I am a blasted shadow
I am nothing but love

With my now perfect hands
I reach down to the living

Peel your footprints from the soil

Toss them like coins
Into the rolling thunder

RECREATING A MIRACULOUS OBJECT

Thus I perish in amazement
At the ruthless curve of your delicate hip

Thus I perish in amazement
At the suggestion of your wrists

Thus I perish in amazement
And am recreated by the aloe of your eyes

Thus I perish in amazement
In your tongue's candied skull

Thus I perish in amazement
Drowning beneath your flowering feet

Thus I perish in amazement and am preserved
In the formaldehyde of your impossible breast

Thus I perish in amazement
Salted in your blood and consumed with milk

Thus I perish in amazement
Dashed to shreds on the glimmering bergs of your teeth

Thus I perish in amazement
Like a flame devoted

Thus I perish in amazement
In the thundering honey of your wake

Thus I perish in amazement
And sink fathomlessly down with all your masks

Thus I perish in amazement
And am born into your favorite laughter

Thus I perish in amazement
Kissing your elemental hands

Thus I perish in amazement
At the ecstasy of your itinerant breath

Thus I perish in amazement
My bones liberated by your wolves

Thus I perish in amazement
Pinned to the axis of your innumerable eye

Thus I perish in amazement
At the matrix of all possible narratives

Thus I perish in amazement
In the mushroom of your every deadly atom

Thus I perish in amazement
A sobbing angel hung in a tree

Thus I perish in amazement
An azure column touching the alabaster sky

Thus I perish in amazement
Plucked like a berry from your trellis of blood

Thus I perish in amazement
In the ribbed lightning of the next great ice age

Thus I perish in amazement
Am magma

Thus I perish in amazement
Am lice

Thus I perish in amazement
As the flowers sway in myriad lysergic awe

Thus I perish in amazement
As you wasp the abyss between my ribs

Thus I perish in amazement
And am made whole by the white mud of your ambivalence

Thus I perish in amazement
Drowning in the black orchard of your hair

Thus I perish in amazement
Eating the poison from your reverential sleep

Thus I perish in amazement
With wings with planets with fingers

Thus I perish in amazement
At the dawn of your surrendered eye breaking on its lid's horizon

Thus I perish in amazement
And am greatest when I know nothing

Thus I perish in amazement
Living for centuries on the freckled hours of your neck

Thus I perish in amazement
Living for centuries on the freckled hours of your neck

Thus I perish in amazement
Strangled by the glorious gesture of your abdomen rising to meet mine

Thus I perish in amazement
Alone in my aberration and still I have not ceased to weep

Thus I perish in amazement
Within the pure lie of mystery we walk

Thus I perish in amazement
My perfect veins crumbling to dust on your fingers' perfect tips

Thus I perish in amazement
The swishing sound and that is enough

Thus I perish in amazement
This rose bursting delicately out then rising

Thus I perish in amazement
A half-open door in a glass of darkness

Thus I perish in amazement
In the gruesomeness of your embrace which no one can take from me

Thus I perish in amazement
Amid the uncurling tides of your wandering

Thus I perish in amazement
Broken by the enormity of a future apart

Thus I perish in amazement
And return to rest my head on your immortal thigh

Thus I perish in amazement
And become the sapling tree that

Centuries from now still bends in the wind
Of your uncertain longing

Thus I perish in amazement
Thus I perish thus I perish still I have not yet ceased to perish

RECREATING A MIRACULOUS OBJECT

In spite of fire and greatness
And the frigid cold

In spite of well water and bread crumbs

In spite of a mother's empty cave

In spite of houses and their failure to house

In spite of a room full of stepladders
And no sleep before dawn

In spite of green arthritic rocks and jagged hands

In spite of mutilated trees at nightfall

In spite of night

In spite of three hundred years
Dissolving into sea foam

In spite of God's dice Manhattan
And the atomic bomb

In spite of fear and trembling toward salvation

In spite of fire

In spite of greatness

In spite of nothing

In spite of a part of us remaining
Wherever we have been

In spite of washcloths and pillows

In spite of the only thing worse than death
Being to live forever

In spite of the perfection of every wall
Of every cell
In my body

In spite of the bright red sun in the pale blue sky

In spite of the bullet wound on a jaguar made of ice

In spite of nothing which is not perfect

In spite of the immortal second

In spite of a door opening to white magnesium fire

In spite of hours

In spite of days

In spite of years

In spite of my flesh colored shadow I have no arms to hold

In spite of that impossible departure

A throne of birds

We unlearn ourselves on every wing

In spite of a place inside so other
We would do anything to escape

In spite of squatting inside a termite's skull

In spite of bat's blood
And the dandruff of angels

In spite of the liquid of all your absences
Seeping into every opened pore you've kissed

In spite of quiet
The sleeping mystery of your mirror

And the emptiness of my eternal approach

In spite of the rough echo of burning stars
Moonlight tilting

Against the sleeping windmill of your lashes

In spite of nothing more still
Than the singing blade

In the kitchen the knife hanging
A lullaby from your mother's lips

In spite of being the fever child of a thousand tentacled dreams
In spite of being the curious child of nothing wonder light

In spite of me beast child in the waking dream
Animal child lightning child pyramid child

In spite of me the black horned fossil child
Of rain and thunder

Monkey child with lightning laughter
Viral child of the bitten bright heart

In spite of giving myself over to fire
In spite of giving the raccoons my dove's eggs

Teeth ringed palm child of night alarmed light
Living child at the edge of hive

In spite of me awake alive
Bright child of fright

In spite of the saint child within me
Feeding the hours my breath

In spite of being clean
Aware and unaware

In spite of finding my reflection in your teeth
In spite of traveling as a ghost

In spite of being a virus wrapped in skin
An effigy of empty acts burning

In spite of me the seed of disorder

In spite of being a mountain
And married to the dead

In spite of working in my sleep
And only appearing in dreams

In spite of the naked decay
Of black matter bending everything around it inwards

The tragedy that is an end to questions

In spite of knowing the end of gloom
In spite of practicing gratitude with every little breath

I practice gratitude I practice gratitude

In spite of death
Death death above and below

Death morning death grass death table death chair
Death death death hello

In spite of the wasp behind the wall of sleep
The religion of the insect shore

The tusk of honey
Piercing the hum of ah

In spite of casting off the house that claimed my life
And making my home in the forever

Opening outward of the other body
In spite of dwelling on that impossible horizon

Where the abyss stars me upward
Into a heaven of limitless light

I am recreated

Printed in the USA
CPSIA information can be obtained
at www.ICGtesting.com
JSHW021344040624
64299JS00004B/210